RECORDED VERSIONS GUITAR

AUTHENTIC TRANSCRIPTIONS
WITH NOTES AND TABLATURE

FIVE FINGER DEATH PUNCH

AMERICAN CAPITALIST

Music transcriptions by Pete Billmann

ISBN 978-1-4584-2129-6

HAL•LEONARD®
CORPORATION

7777 W. BLUEMOUND RD. P.O. BOX 13819 MILWAUKEE, WI 53213

Visit Hal Leonard Online at
www.halleonard.com

American Capitalist

Words and Music by Ivan Moody, Jeremy Spencer, Thomas Jason Grinstead, Zoltan Bathory and Kevin Churko

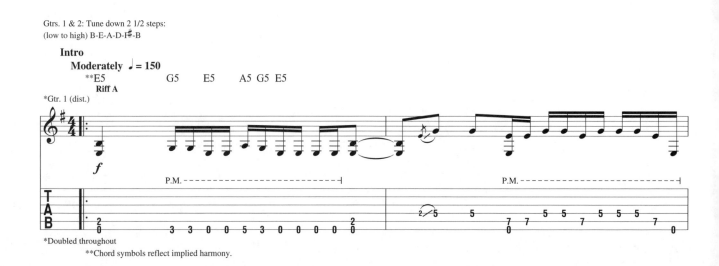

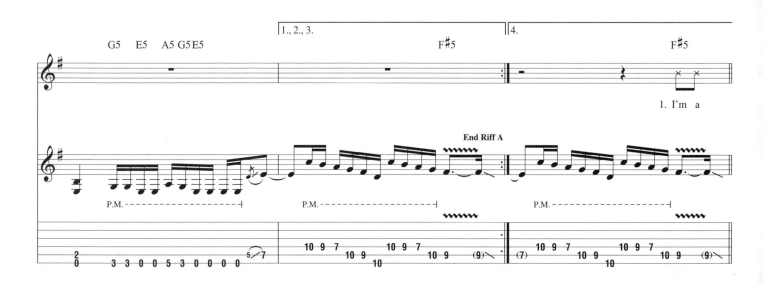

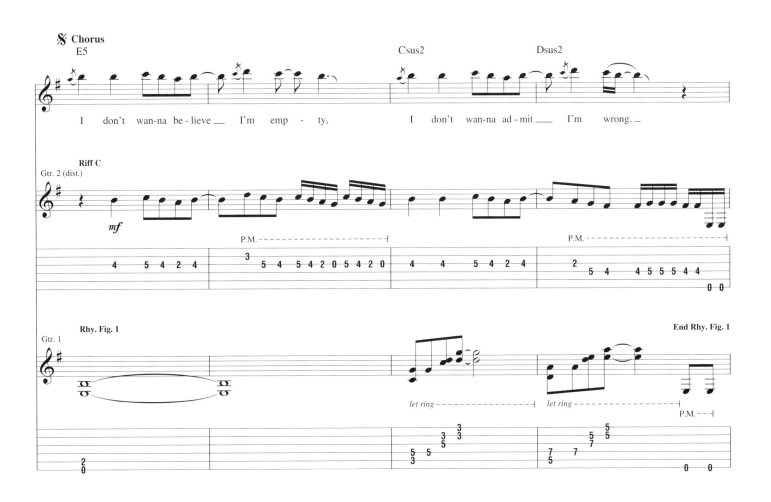

*Ld. voc.: w/ echo set for whole-note
regeneration w/ 1 repeat, next 8 meas.

3

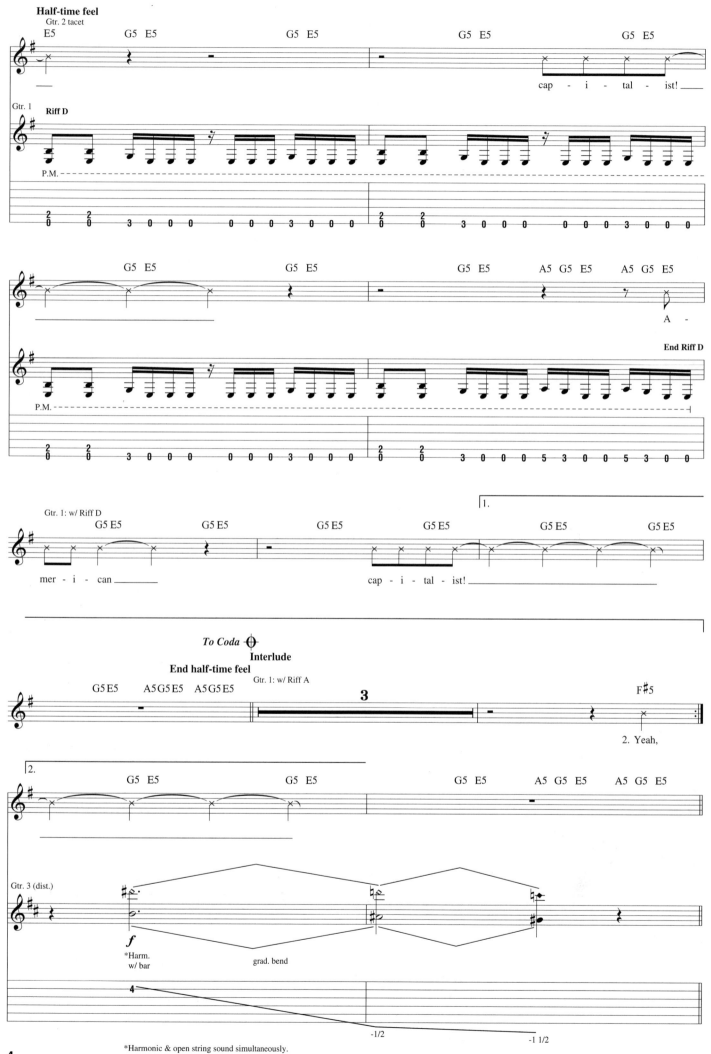

Guitar Solo

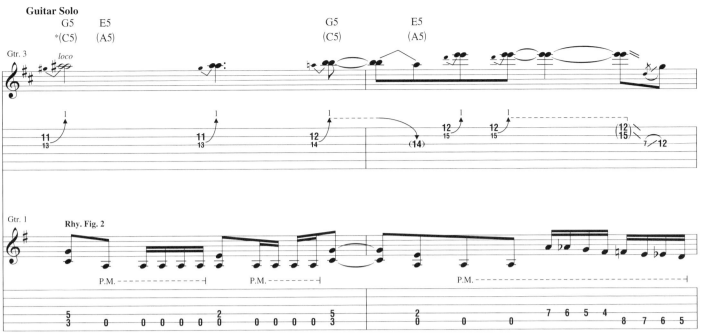

*Symbols in parentheses represent chord names respective to detuned guitar.
Symbols above reflect actual sounding chords.

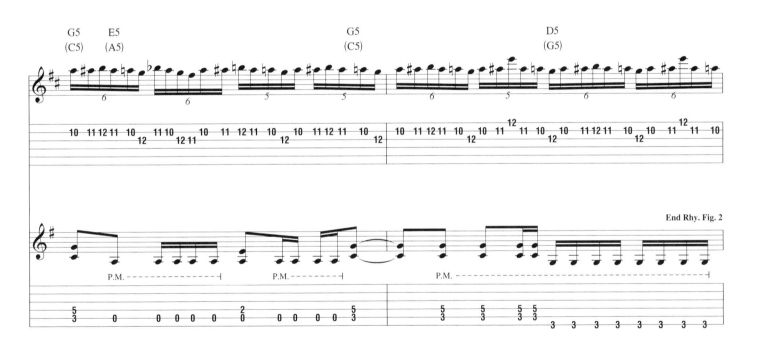

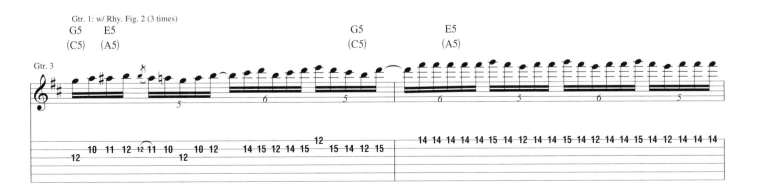

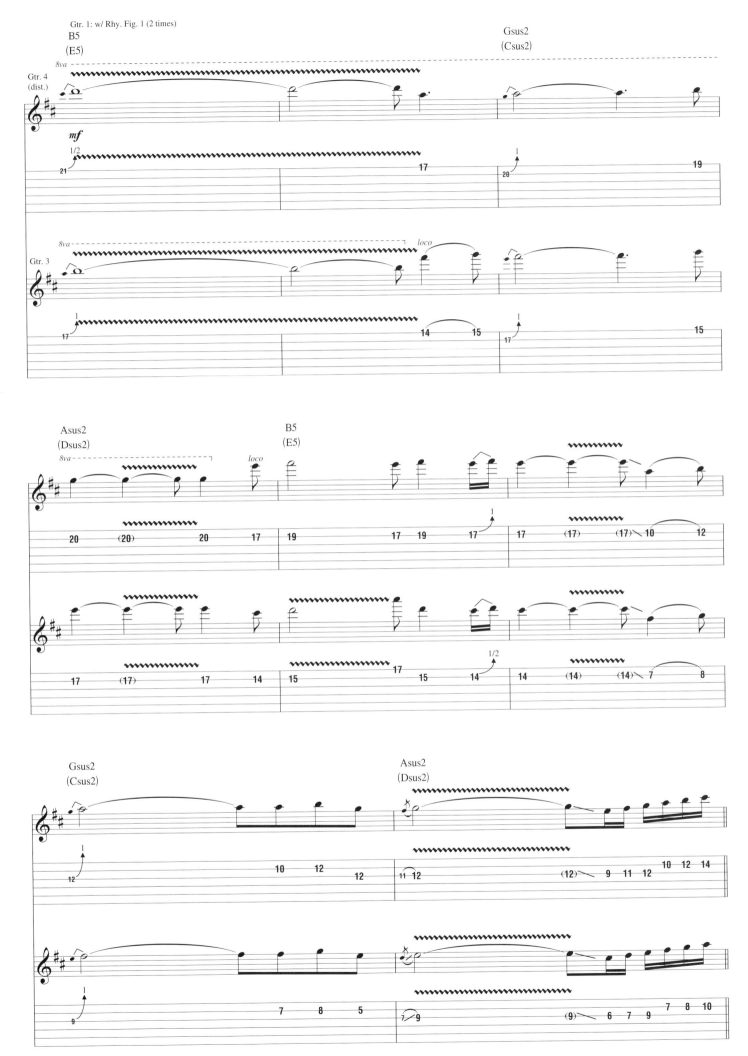

Under and Over It

Words and Music by Ivan Moody, Jeremy Spencer, Thomas Jason Grinstead, Zoltan Bathory and Kevin Churko

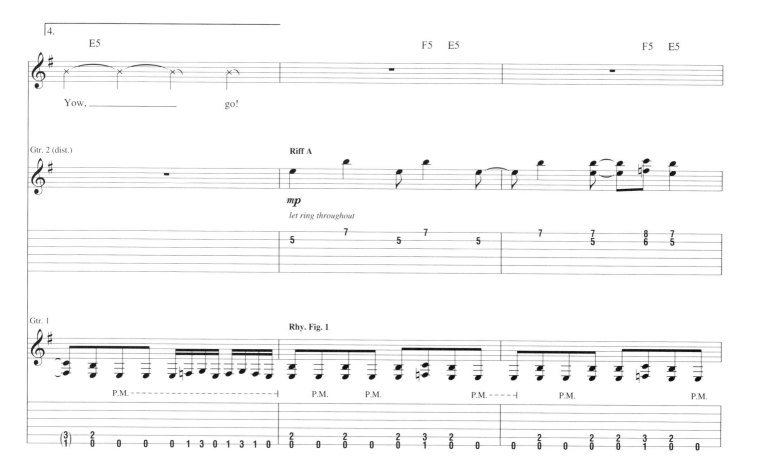

% Chorus

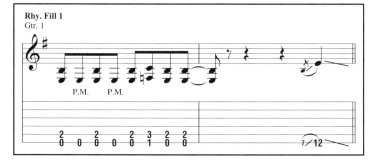

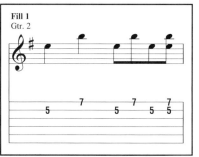

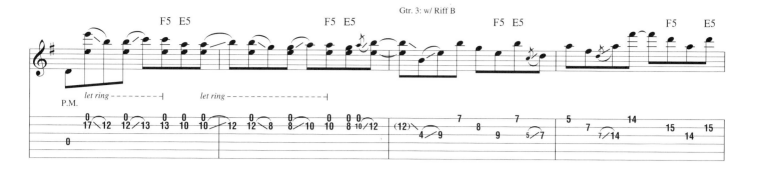

Half-time feel

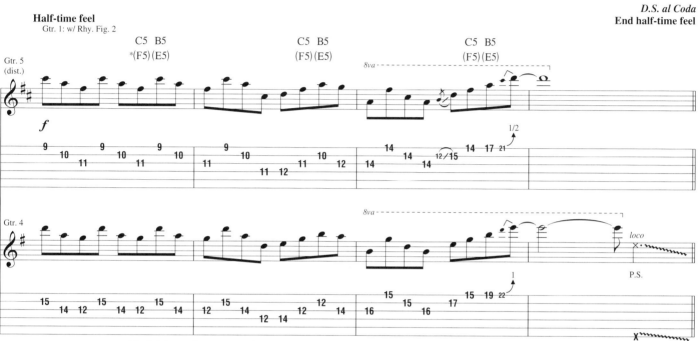

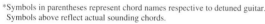

*Symbols in parentheses represent chord names respective to detuned guitar.
Symbols above reflect actual sounding chords.

⊕ Coda

The Pride

Words and Music by Ivan Moody, Jeremy Spencer, Thomas Jason Grinstead, Zoltan Bathory and Kevin Churko

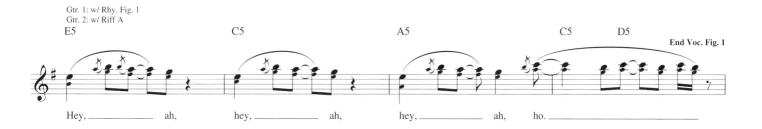

Gtr. 1: w/ Rhy. Fig. 1
Gtr. 2: w/ Riff A

E5   C5   A5   C5   D5

End Voc. Fig. 1

Hey, _____ ah, hey, _____ ah, hey, _____ ah, ho. _____

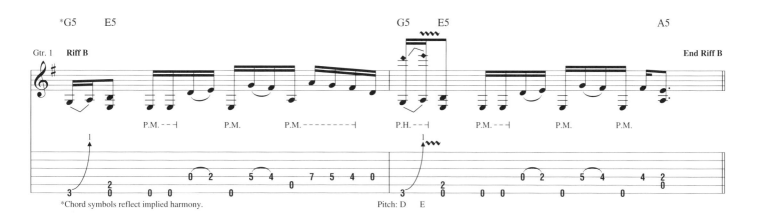

*G5 E5   G5 E5   A5

Gtr. 1 **Riff B**   **End Riff B**

P.M.   P.M.   P.M.   P.H.   P.M.   P.M.   P.M.

*Chord symbols reflect implied harmony.   Pitch: D E

Verse

G5 E5   G5   E5

1. John-ny Cash and P. B. R., Jack Dan-iels, NAS - CAR. Face - book, My - space, i - Pod, Bill Gates.
2. Dis-ney-land, White House, J. F. K. and Mick-ey Mouse. John Wayne, Spring - steen, East - wood, James Dean.

Riff C   **End Riff C**

P.M.   P.M.   P.M.   P.M.   P.M.   P.M.

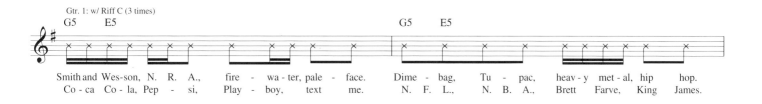

Gtr. 1: w/ Riff C (3 times)

G5 E5   G5   E5

Smith and Wes-son, N. R. A., fire - wa-ter, pale - face. Dime - bag, Tu - pac, heav - y met - al, hip hop.
Co - ca Co - la, Pep - si, Play - boy, text me. N. F. L., N. B. A., Brett Farve, King James.

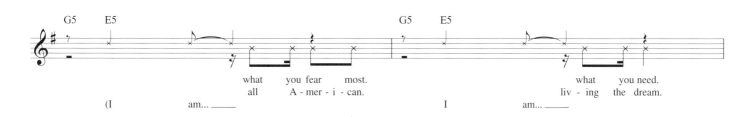

G5 E5   G5 E5

what you fear most.   what you need.
all A - mer - i - can.   liv - ing the dream.

(I am... _____   I am... _____

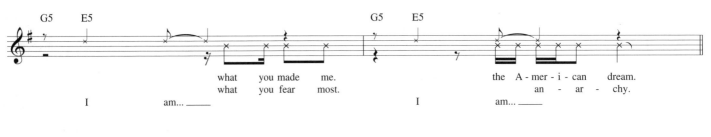

G5   E5

what you made me.
what you fear most.
I am...
the A-mer-i-can dream.
an-ar-chy.
I am...

Pre-Chorus

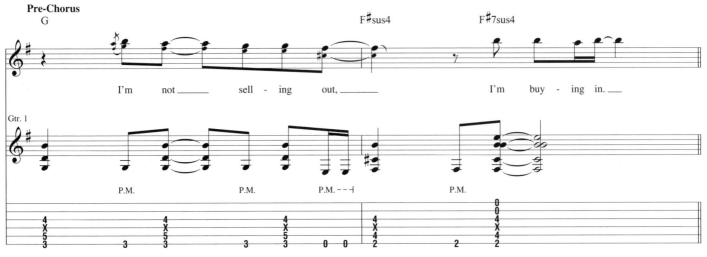

G

F#sus4   F#7sus4

I'm not sell-ing out, I'm buy-ing in.

Gtr. 1

P.M.   P.M.   P.M.---   P.M.

Chorus

Bkgd. Voc.: w/ Voc. Fig. 1
Gtr. 1: w/ Rhy. Fig. 1 (2 times)
Gtr. 2: w/ Riff A (2 times)

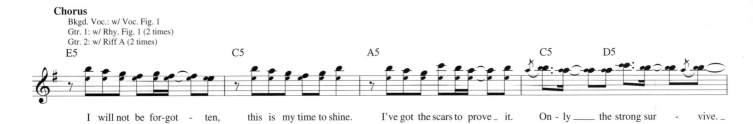

E5   C5   A5   C5   D5

I will not be for-got - ten, this is my time to shine. I've got the scars to prove it. On - ly the strong sur - vive.

E5   C5   A5   C5   D5

I'm not a-fraid of dy - ing, ev-'ry-one has their time. Life nev-er fa-vored weak - ness. Wel-come to the pride.

1.

Interlude

Gtr. 1: w/ Riff C   Gtr. 1: w/ Riff B
G5 E5   G5 E5   G5 E5   G5 E5   A5

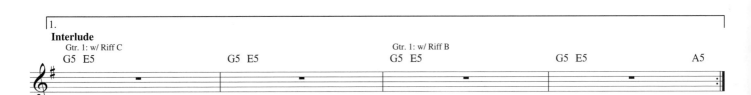

2.

Interlude

E5   F5 E5   F5 D5/A E5   F5 E5   F5 D5/A E5   F5 E5   F5 D5/A

Spoken: Since the dawn of time,
Rhy. Fig. 2

Gtr. 1

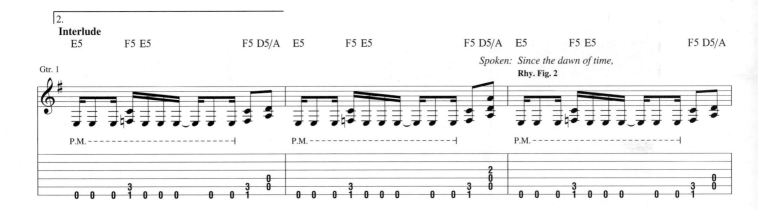

P.M. - - - - - - - - -   P.M. - - - - - - - - -   P.M. - - - - - - - - -

16

Guitar Solo

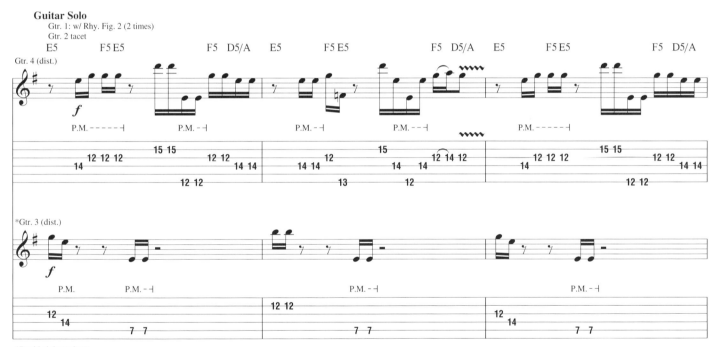

*Doubled throughout

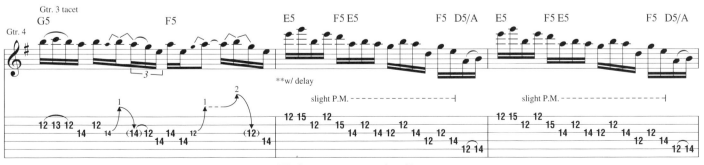

**w/ delay

**Set for quarter-note regeneration w/ 3 repeats.

Interlude

Bkgd. Voc.: w/ Voc. Fig. 1
Gtr. 1: w/ Rhy. Fig. 1 (2 times)
Gtr. 2: w/ Riff A (2 times)
Gtr. 4 tacet

(Oh, _____ oh. _____

_____ Oh, _____ oh.) _____

On - ly _____ the strong sur - vive! _____

Wel - come _____ to _____ the pride!

Chorus

Bkgd. Voc.: w/ Voc. Fig. 1
Gtr. 1: w/ Rhy. Fig. 1 (1 1/2 times)
Gtr. 2: w/ Riff A (2 times)

I will not be for - got - ten, this is my time to shine. I've got the scars to prove _____ it.

On - ly _____ the strong sur - vive. _____ I'm not a - fraid of dy - ing, ev - 'ry - one has their time.

Life nev - er fa - vored weak - ness. Wel - come _____ to _____ the pride. _____

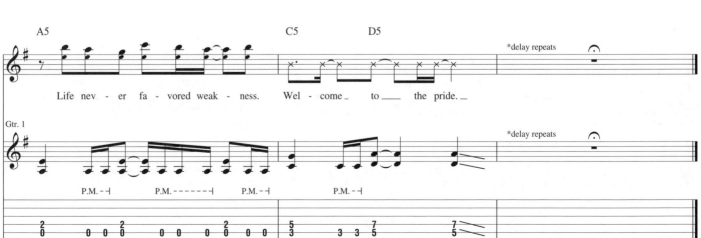

*Effect encompasses entire mix.

Coming Down

Words and Music by Ivan Moody, Jeremy Spencer, Thomas Jason Grinstead, Zoltan Bathory and Kevin Churko

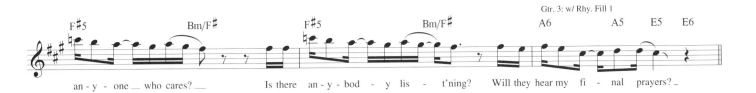

an-y-one ___ who cares? ___ Is there an-y-bod ___ -y lis ___ -t'ning? Will they hear my fi ___ -nal prayers? ___

D.S. al Coda 1

Pre-Chorus
Gtrs. 1 & 2: w/ Rhy. Fig. 1

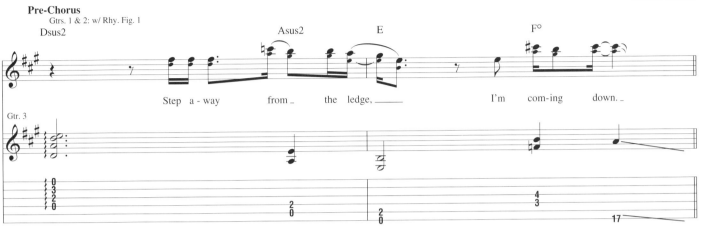

Step a-way from ___ the ledge, ___ I'm com-ing down. ___

⊕ **Coda 1**

Bridge

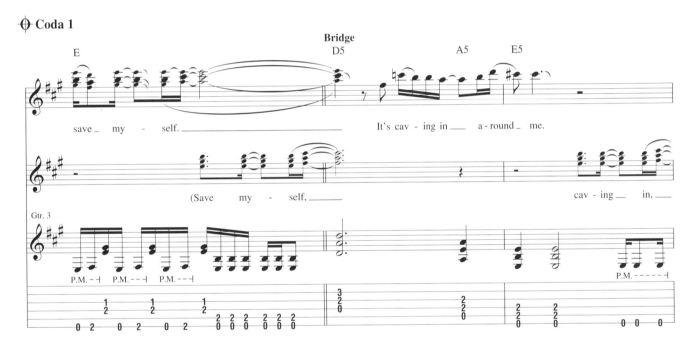

save ___ my - self. ___ It's cav-ing in ___ a-round ___ me.

(Save my - self, ___ cav-ing ___ in, ___

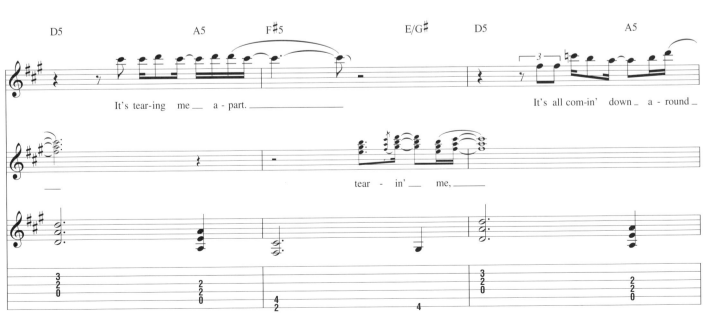

It's tear-ing me ___ a-part. It's all com-in' down ___ a-round ___

tear - in' ___ me, ___

23

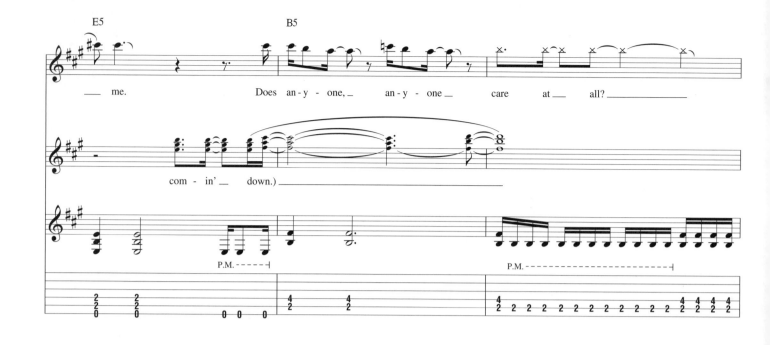

me. Does an-y-one,_ an-y-one_ care at _ all? _____

com - in' _ down.) _____

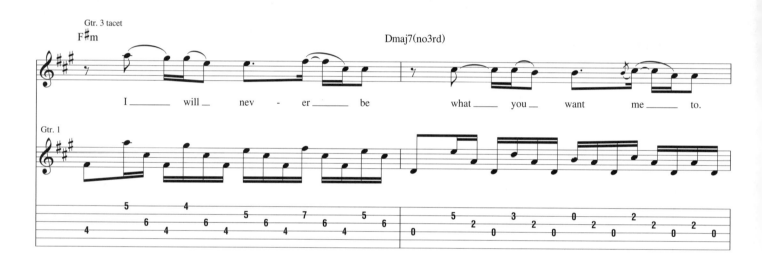

I _ will _ nev - er _ be what _ you _ want me _ to.

You pull me un-der, I pull you un - der.

*Vol. swell

Interlude

*Symbols in parantheses represent chord names respective to detuned guitar.
Symbols above reflect actual sounding chords.

Guitar Solo

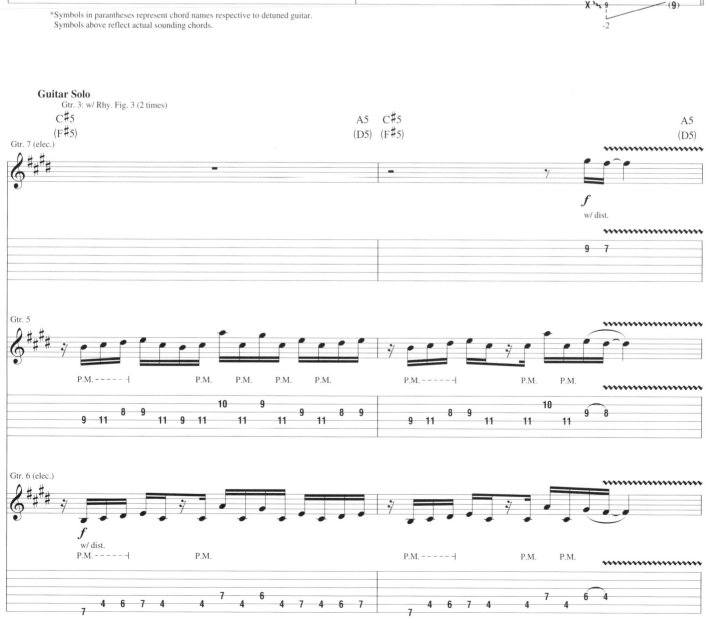

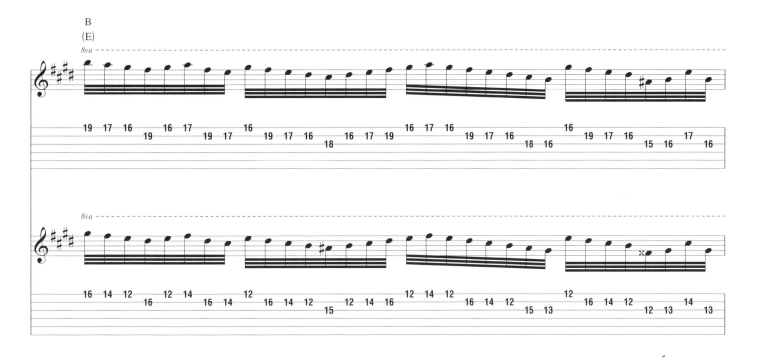

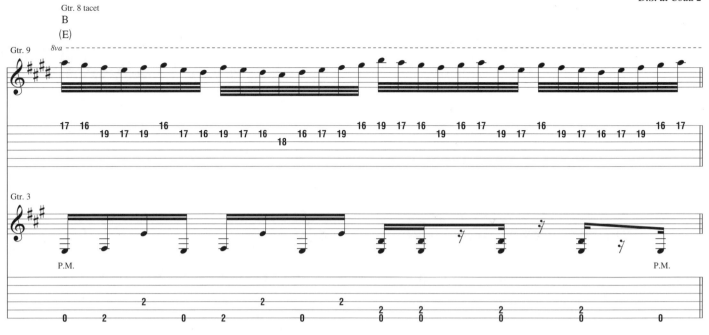

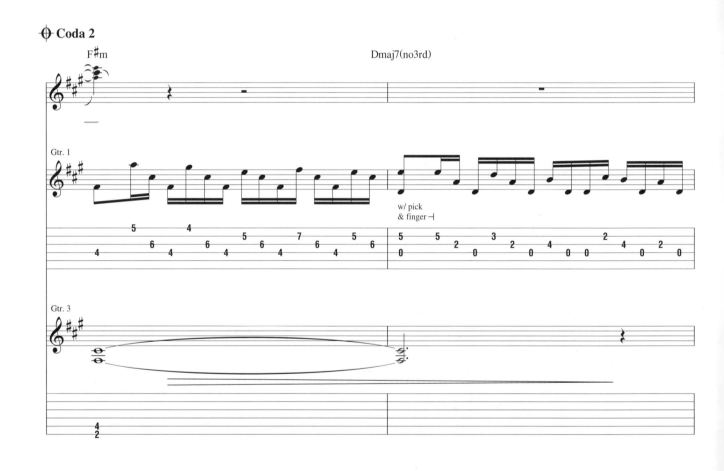

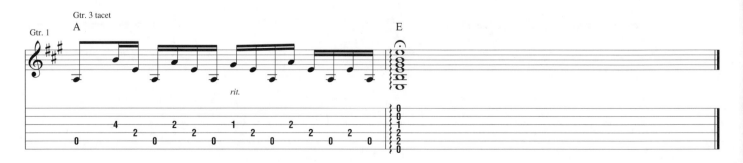

Menace

Words and Music by Ivan Moody, Jeremy Spencer, Thomas Jason Grinstead and Zoltan Bathory

Generation Dead

Words and Music by Ivan Moody, Jeremy Spencer, Thomas Jason Grinstead, Zoltan Bathory and Kevin Churko

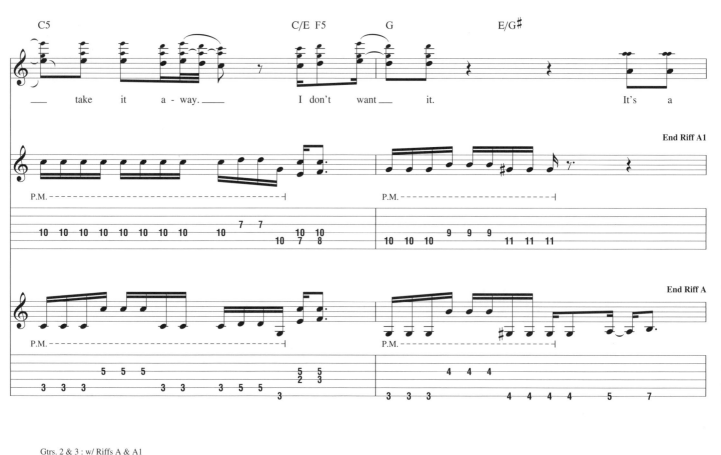

take it a-way. ___ I don't want ___ it. It's a

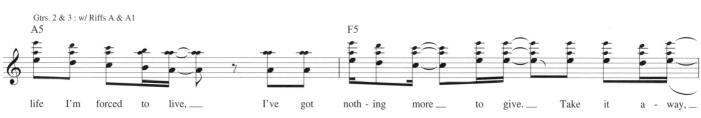

life I'm forced to live, ___ I've got noth-ing more ___ to give. ___ Take it a - way, ___

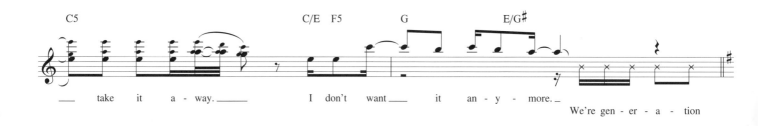

take it a-way. ___ I don't want ___ it an-y-more. ___ We're gen-er-a-tion

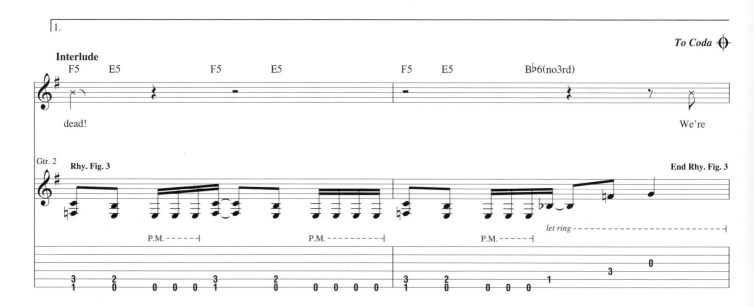

dead! We're

*Symbols in parentheses represent chord names respective to detuned guitar.
 Symbols above reflect actual sounding chords.

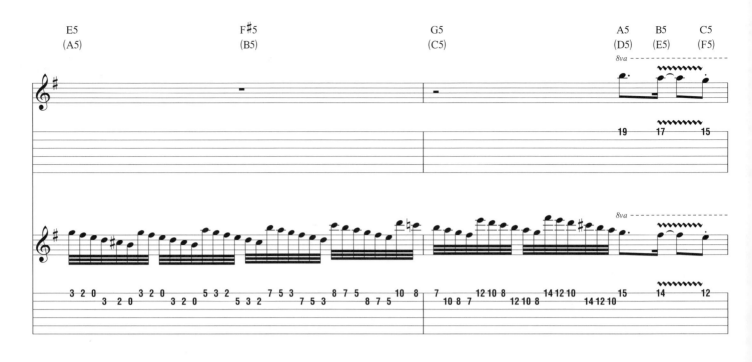

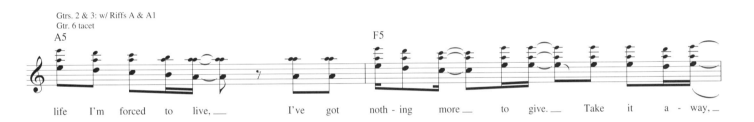

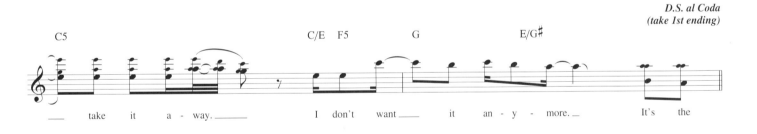

Back for More

Words and Music by Ivan Moody, Jeremy Spencer, Thomas Jason Grinstead, Zoltan Bathory and Kevin Churko

Gtrs. 1-4: Tune down 2 1/2 steps:
(low to high) B-E-A-D-F#-B

Intro
Moderately fast ♩ = 153

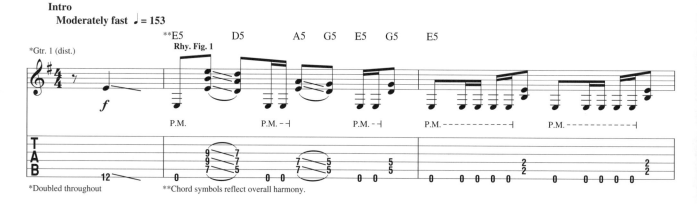

*Doubled throughout   **Chord symbols reflect overall harmony.

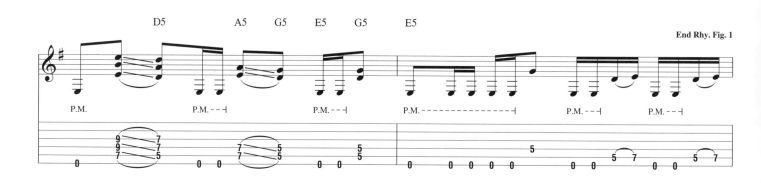

1. Let's get it

Verse

***w/ echo set for dotted quarter-note regeneration w/ 1 repeat.

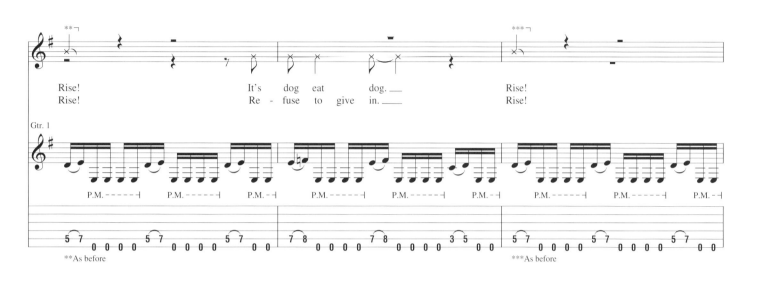

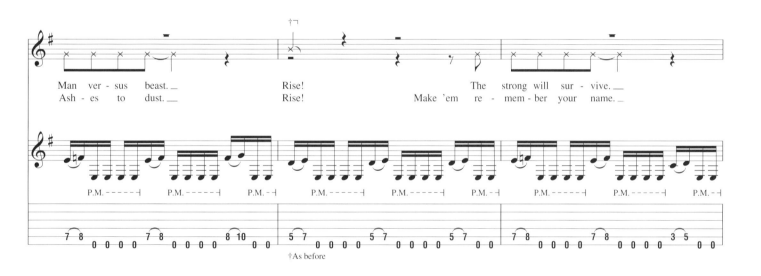

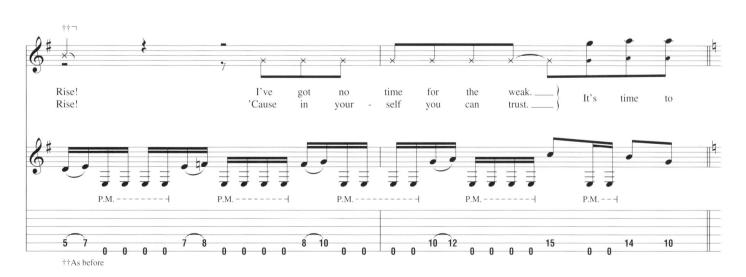

§ **Chorus**

3rd time, Gtr. 5: w/ Fill 1

rise up, man up, get back _ up. Nev - er been and won't _ be bro - ken.

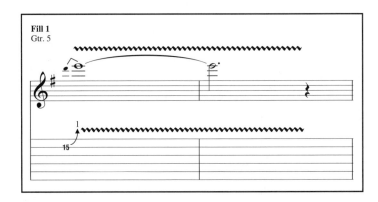

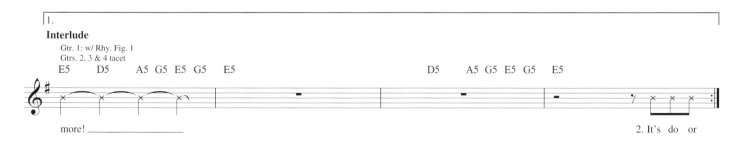

2.

To Coda ⊕

Interlude
Half-time feel

*Symbols in parentheses represent chord names respective to detuned guitar.
Symbols above reflect actual sounding chords.

Guitar Solo

End half-time feel

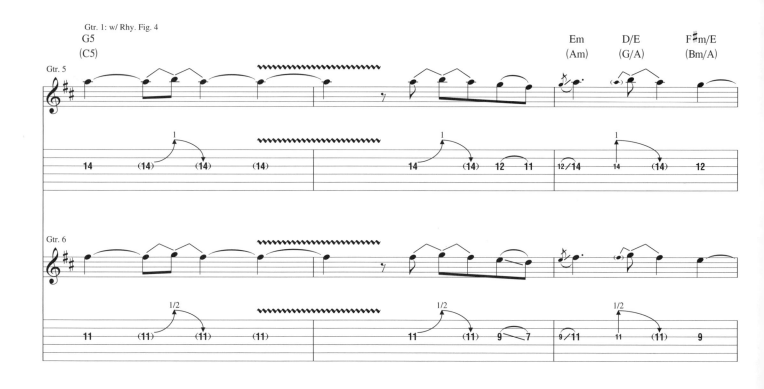

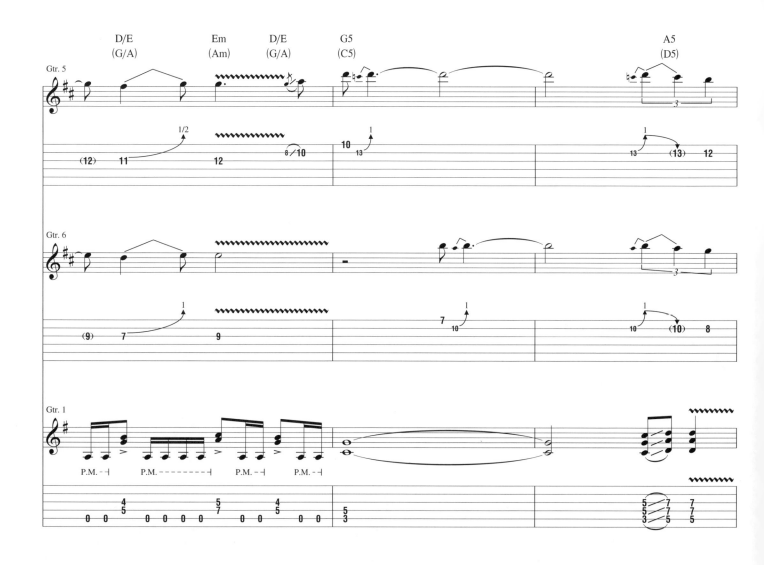

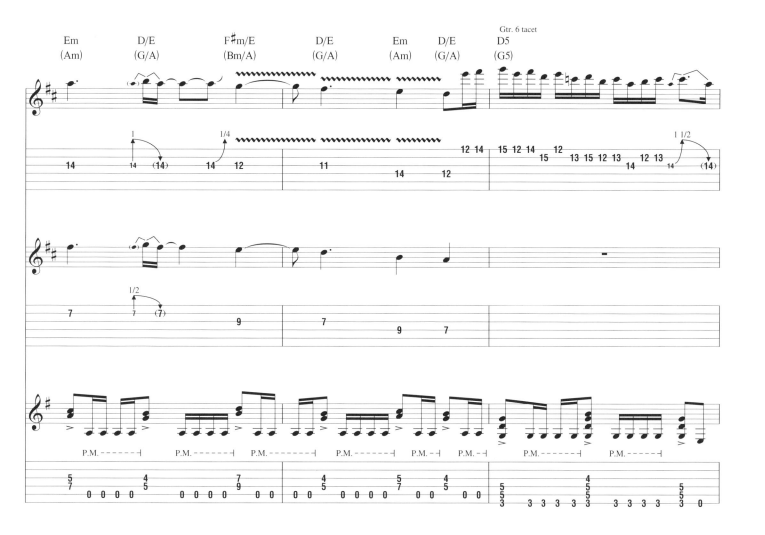

Coda

D.S. al Coda
(take 2nd ending)

It's time to

Rah!

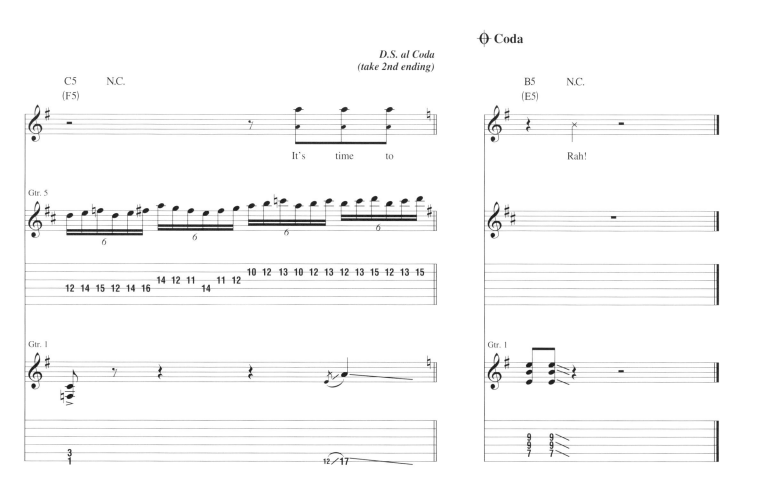

Remember Everything

Words and Music by Ivan Moody, Jeremy Spencer, Thomas Jason Grinstead, Zoltan Bathory, Kevin Churko and Kane Churko

Gtrs. 1-4: Drop D tuning, down 2 1/2 steps:
(low to high) A-E-A-D-F#-B

*Chord symbols reflect implied harmony.
**Vol. swell

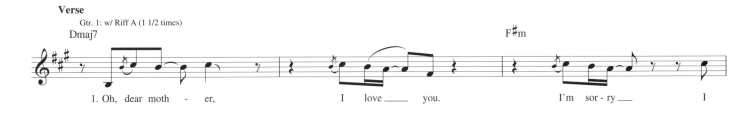

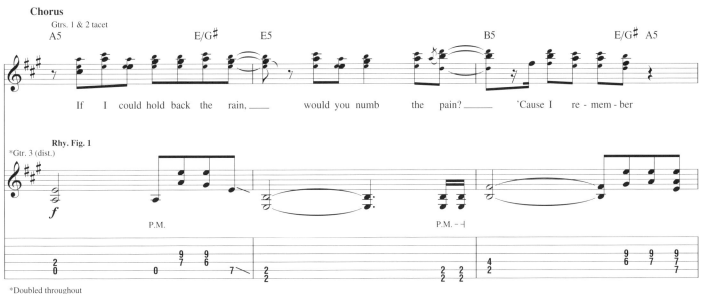

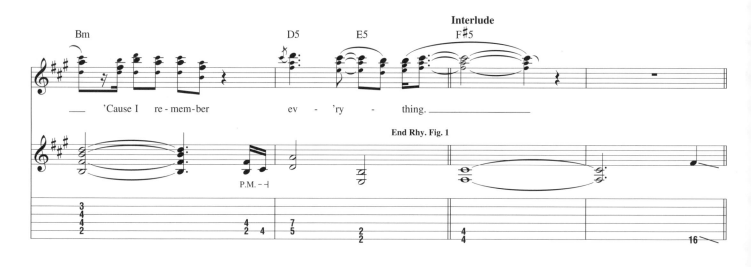

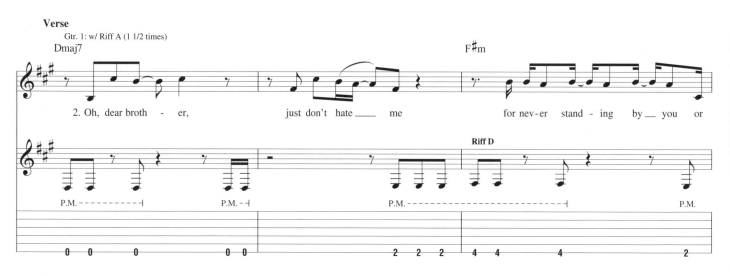

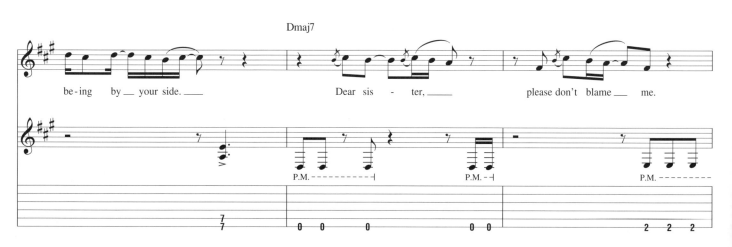

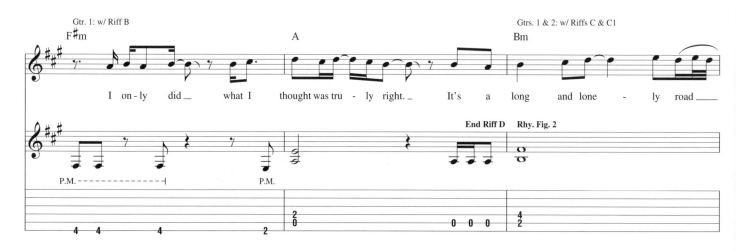

when you know you walk a - lone.

End Rhy. Fig. 2

P.M.

Chorus

Gtr. 3: w/ Rhy. Fig. 1

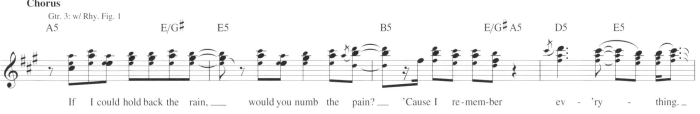

If I could hold back the rain, would you numb the pain? 'Cause I re-mem-ber ev - 'ry - thing.

If I could help you for - get, would you take my re-grets? 'Cause I re-mem-ber ev - 'ry - thing.

Bridge

I feel like run-nin' a - way, I'm still so far from home. You say that I'll nev-er change, but what the fuck do you know?

Gtr. 4 (dist.)

mf

let ring throughout

Gtr. 3

P.M.

*w/ echo set for quarter-note
regeneration w/ 5 repeats.

I'll burn it all to the ground before I let you in. Please forgive me, I can't forgive you now.

Interlude

Gtr. 1: w/ Riff A (1st 2 meas.)
Gtrs. 3 & 4 tacet

I remember ev'rything.

Guitar Solo

Gtr. 1: w/ Riff A (last 2 meas.)
Gtr. 3: w/ Riff D

Gtr. 1: w/ Riff A (1st 2 meas.)

**Symbols in parentheses represent chord names respective to detuned guitar.
Symbols above reflect actual sounding chords.

Gtr. 1: w/ Riff B

Gtrs. 1 & 2: w/ Riffs C & C1
Gtr. 3: w/ Rhy. Fig. 2

Wicked Ways

Words and Music by Ivan Moody, Jeremy Spencer, Thomas Jason Grinstead, Zoltan Bathory and Kevin Churko

Gtrs. 1 & 2: w/ Riff A

Bb5 E5   Bb5 E5   Bb5 E5   D5 E5   F5 E5 F5 E5   D5 E5 D5   E5   F5

1. I should have

Verse

Gtrs. 1 & 2: w/ Riff A (2 times)

Bb5   E5   Bb5   E5   Bb5   E5

seen _____ this   from a mile a - way. _ I should have nev-er let _ you get that deep _ in - side. _
vi - rus   that's spread through-out _ my veins, _ you're in - cur - a - ble _ and such a waste _ of time. _

D5 E5   F5 E5 F5 E5   D5 E5 D5 E5   F5   Bb5   E5   Bb5   E5

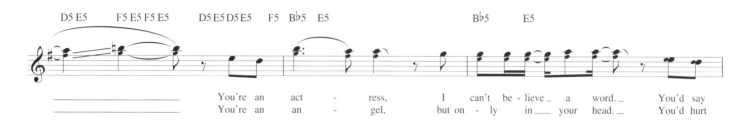

_____ You're an act - ress,   I can't be - lieve _ a word. _ You'd say
_____ You're an an - gel,   but on - ly in ___ your head. _ You'd hurt

Bb5   E5   D5 E5   F5 E5 F5 E5   D5 E5 D5 E5   F5

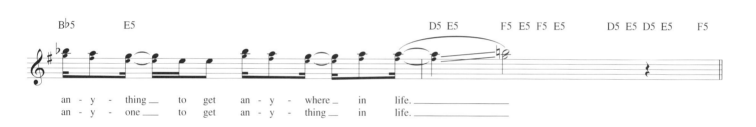

an - y - thing _ to get an - y - where _ in life. _____
an - y - one ___ to get an - y - thing _ in life. _____

Pre-Chorus

G5   A5   F#5

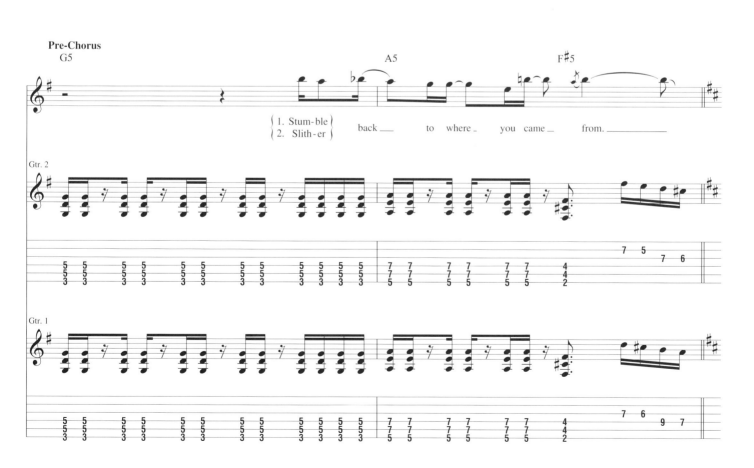

{1. Stum-ble} back ___ to where _ you came _ from. _____
{2. Slith-er}

Gtr. 2

Gtr. 1

57

58

If I Fall

Words and Music by Ivan Moody, Jeremy Spencer, Thomas Jason Grinstead, Zoltan Bathory and Kevin Churko

Gtrs. 1-6: Tune down 2 1/2 steps:
(low to high) B-E-A-D-F#-B

Intro
Moderately fast ♩ = 160
Half-time feel

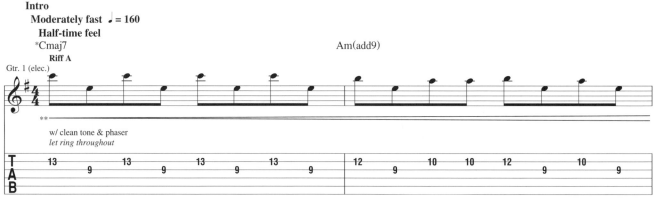

*Chord symbols reflect implied harmony.
**Track fades in.

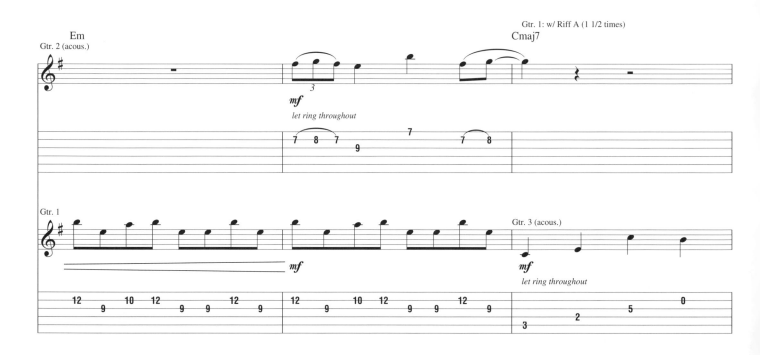

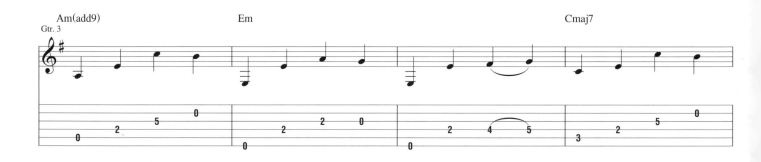

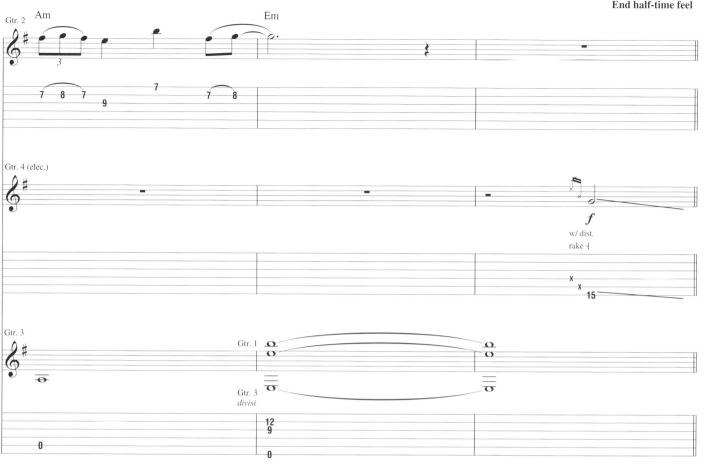

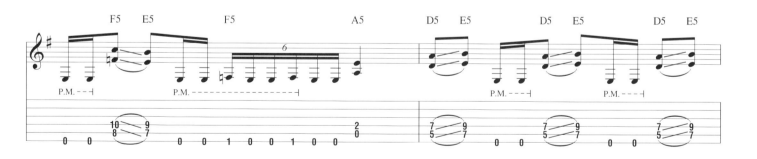

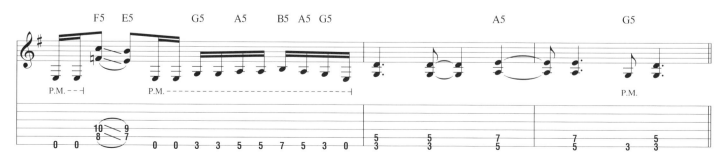

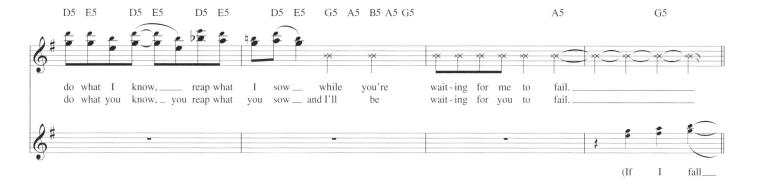

do what I know,____ reap what I sow__ while you're waiting for me to fail. ____
do what you know,__ you reap what you sow__ and I'll be waiting for you to fail. ____

(If I fall__

% **Chorus**
Half-time feel

3rd time, Gtr. 9 tacet

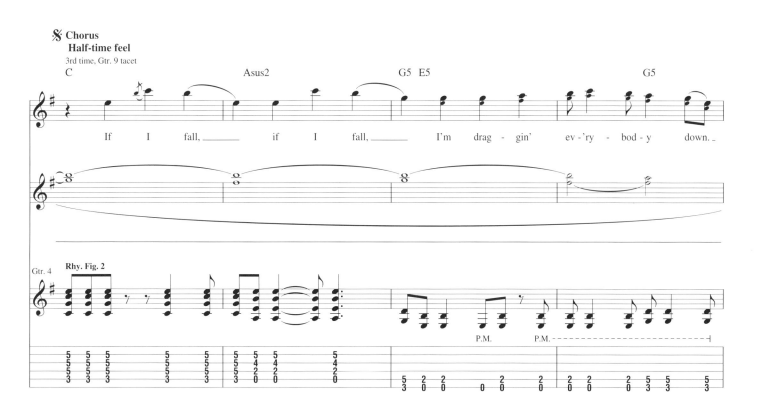

If I fall, ____ if I fall, ____ I'm drag-gin' ev-'ry-bod-y down._

If I fall, ____ I will... (Take ev-'ry-bod-y down.) ____

__ if I fall.)____

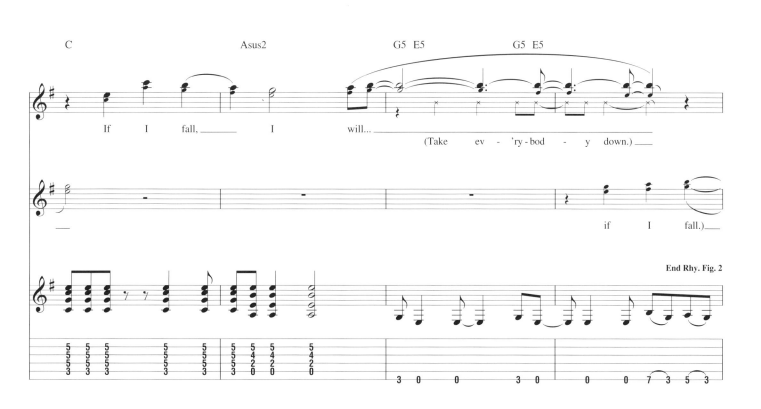

Gtrs. 1 & 4: w/ Riffs B & B1
Gtr. 5 tacet

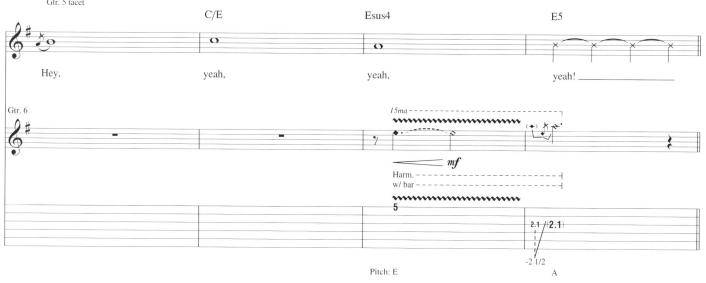

Pitch: E

Bridge

Gtr. 4: w/ Riff B (4 times)
Gtr. 6 tacet

*Symbols in parentheses represent chord names respective to detuned guitar.
Symbols above reflect actual sounding chords.

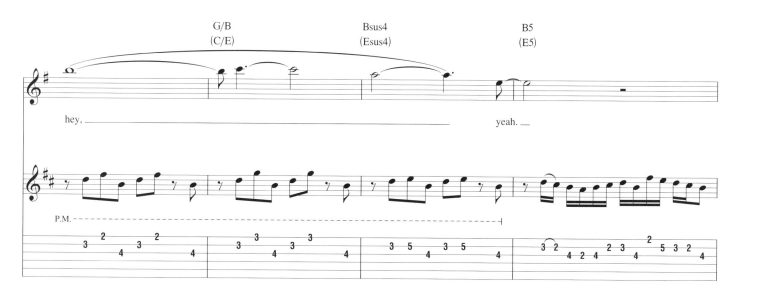

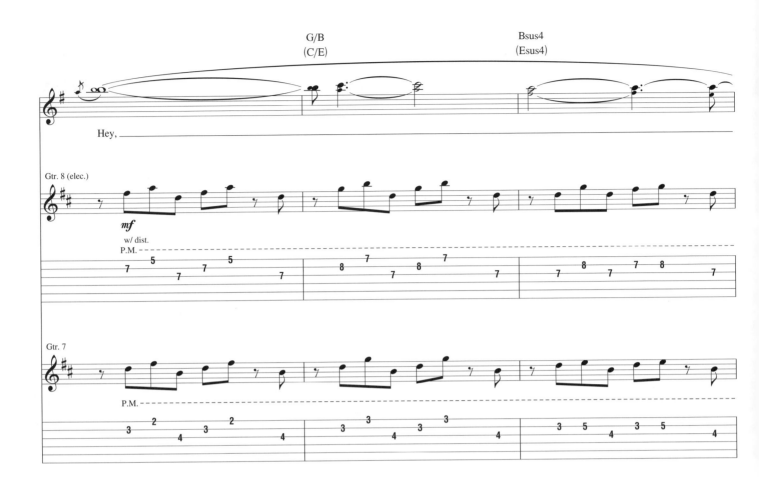

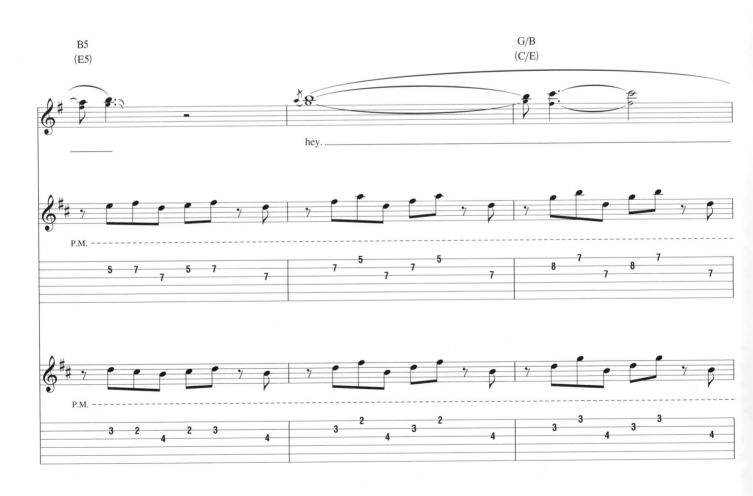

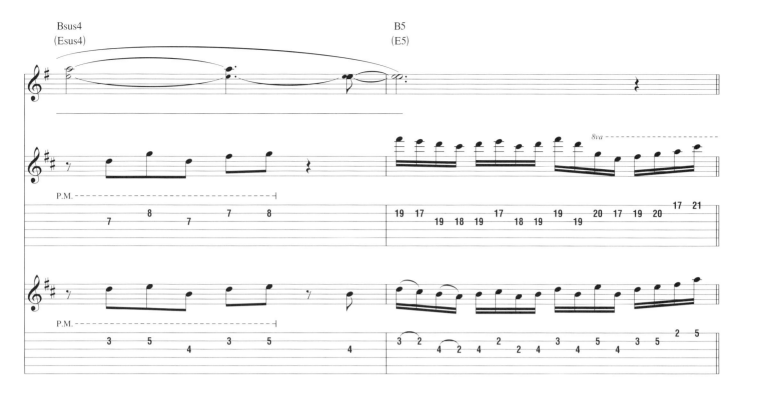

Interlude

If I fall, _____ if I fall, I'm tak - in' ev - 'ry - bod - y down.

*Piano arr. for gtr.

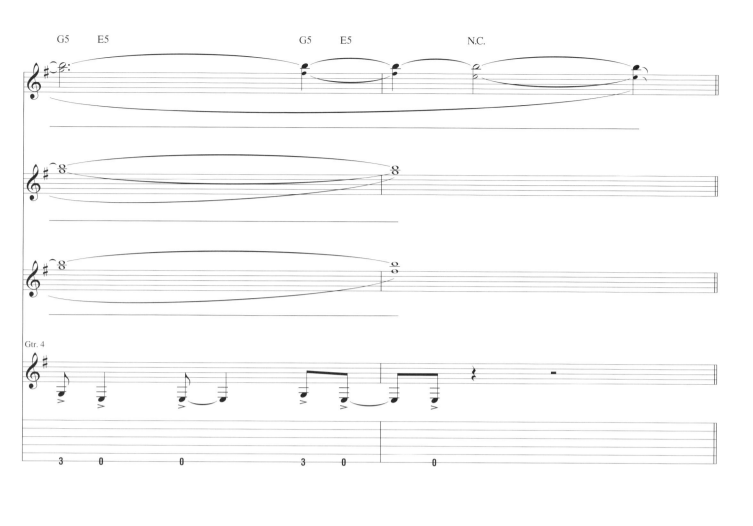

Outro

Gtr. 4 tacet

Cmaj7   Am(add9)   Em

Gtr. 3

Riff C   End Riff C

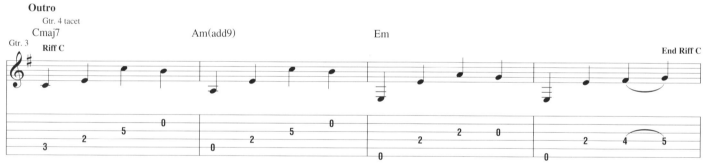

Begin fade

Gtr. 3: w/ Riff C (till fade)

Cmaj7   Am(add9)   Em

Gtr. 2

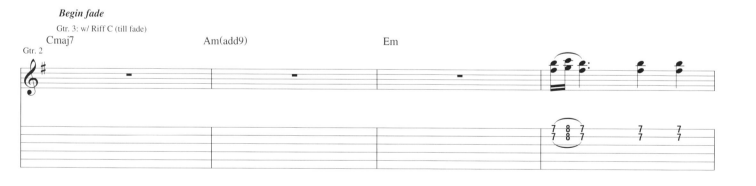

Fade out

Gtr. 2 tacet

Cmaj7   Am(add9)   Em

100 Ways to Hate

Words and Music by Ivan Moody, Jeremy Spencer, Thomas Jason Grinstead, Zoltan Bathory and Kevin Churko

Gtrs. 1, 2 & 3: Tune down 2 1/2 steps:
(low to high) B-E-A-D-F♯-B

*Doubled throughout

**Chord symbols reflect implied harmony.

1. Hate your

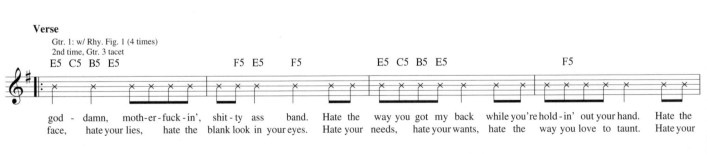

god - damn, moth-er-fuck-in', shit-ty ass band. Hate the way you got my back while you're hold-in' out your hand. Hate the
face, hate your lies, hate the blank look in your eyes. Hate your needs, hate your wants, hate the way you love to taunt. Hate your

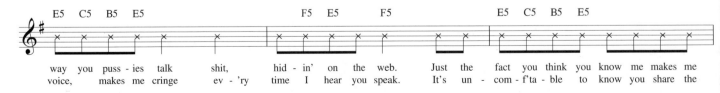

way you puss-ies talk shit, hid-in' on the web. Just the fact you think you know me makes me
voice, makes me cringe ev-'ry time I hear you speak. It's un-com-f'ta-ble to know you share the

*Symbols in parentheses represent chord names respective to detuned guitar.
 Symbols above reflect actual sounding chords.

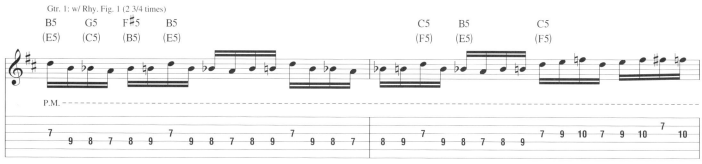

*Played behind the beat.

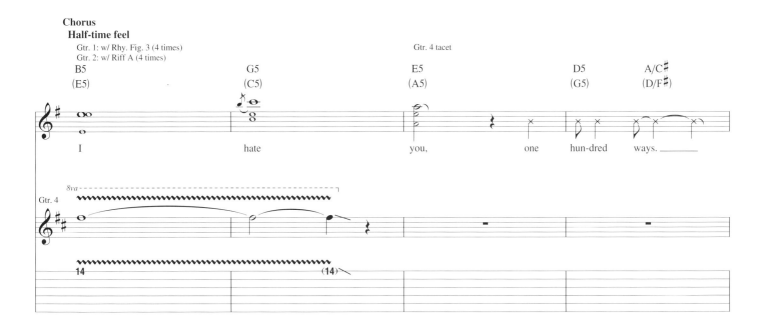

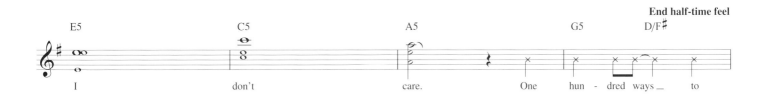

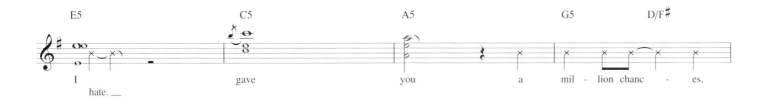

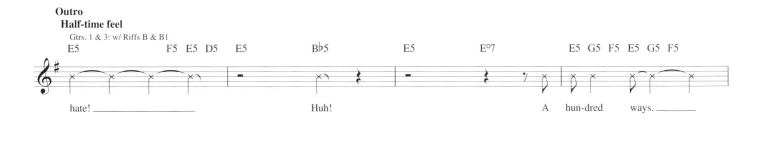

GUITAR NOTATION LEGEND

Guitar music can be notated three different ways: on a *musical staff*, in *tablature*, and in *rhythm slashes*.

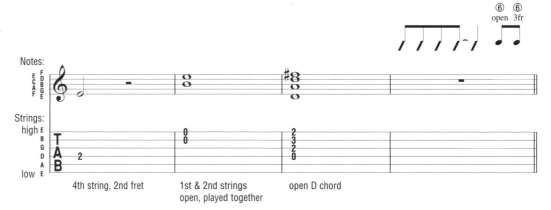

RHYTHM SLASHES are written above the staff. Strum chords in the rhythm indicated. Use the chord diagrams found at the top of the first page of the transcription for the appropriate chord voicings. Round noteheads indicate single notes.

THE MUSICAL STAFF shows pitches and rhythms and is divided by bar lines into measures. Pitches are named after the first seven letters of the alphabet.

TABLATURE graphically represents the guitar fingerboard. Each horizontal line represents a string, and each number represents a fret.

4th string, 2nd fret

1st & 2nd strings open, played together

open D chord

Definitions for Special Guitar Notation

HALF-STEP BEND: Strike the note and bend up 1/2 step.

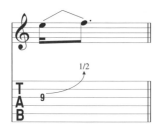

WHOLE-STEP BEND: Strike the note and bend up one step.

GRACE NOTE BEND: Strike the note and immediately bend up as indicated.

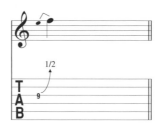

SLIGHT (MICROTONE) BEND: Strike the note and bend up 1/4 step.

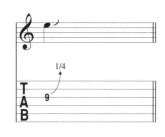

BEND AND RELEASE: Strike the note and bend up as indicated, then release back to the original note. Only the first note is struck.

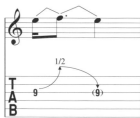

PRE-BEND: Bend the note as indicated, then strike it.

PRE-BEND AND RELEASE: Bend the note as indicated. Strike it and release the bend back to the original note.

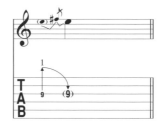

UNISON BEND: Strike the two notes simultaneously and bend the lower note up to the pitch of the higher.

VIBRATO: The string is vibrated by rapidly bending and releasing the note with the fretting hand.

WIDE VIBRATO: The pitch is varied to a greater degree by vibrating with the fretting hand.

HAMMER-ON: Strike the first (lower) note with one finger, then sound the higher note (on the same string) with another finger by fretting it without picking.

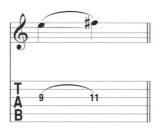

PULL-OFF: Place both fingers on the notes to be sounded. Strike the first note and without picking, pull the finger off to sound the second (lower) note.

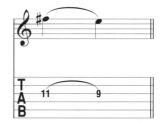

LEGATO SLIDE: Strike the first note and then slide the same fret-hand finger up or down to the second note. The second note is not struck.

SHIFT SLIDE: Same as legato slide, except the second note is struck.

TRILL: Very rapidly alternate between the notes indicated by continuously hammering on and pulling off.

TAPPING: Hammer ("tap") the fret indicated with the pick-hand index or middle finger and pull off to the note fretted by the fret hand.

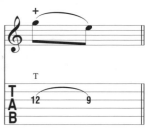

NATURAL HARMONIC: Strike the note while the fret-hand lightly touches the string directly over the fret indicated.

PINCH HARMONIC: The note is fretted normally and a harmonic is produced by adding the edge of the thumb or the tip of the index finger of the pick hand to the normal pick attack.

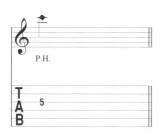

HARP HARMONIC: The note is fretted normally and a harmonic is produced by gently resting the pick hand's index finger directly above the indicated fret (in parentheses) while the pick hand's thumb or pick assists by plucking the appropriate string.

PICK SCRAPE: The edge of the pick is rubbed down (or up) the string, producing a scratchy sound.

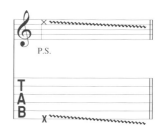

MUFFLED STRINGS: A percussive sound is produced by laying the fret hand across the string(s) without depressing, and striking them with the pick hand.

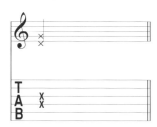

PALM MUTING: The note is partially muted by the pick hand lightly touching the string(s) just before the bridge.

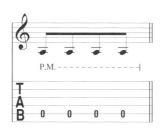

RAKE: Drag the pick across the strings indicated with a single motion.

TREMOLO PICKING: The note is picked as rapidly and continuously as possible.

ARPEGGIATE: Play the notes of the chord indicated by quickly rolling them from bottom to top.

VIBRATO BAR DIVE AND RETURN: The pitch of the note or chord is dropped a specified number of steps (in rhythm), then returned to the original pitch.

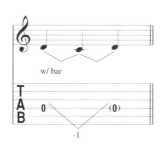

VIBRATO BAR SCOOP: Depress the bar just before striking the note, then quickly release the bar.

VIBRATO BAR DIP: Strike the note and then immediately drop a specified number of steps, then release back to the original pitch.

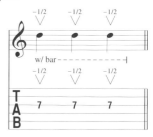

Additional Musical Definitions

(accent)	•	Accentuate note (play it louder).
(accent)	•	Accentuate note with great intensity.
(staccato)	•	Play the note short.
⊓	•	Downstroke
V	•	Upstroke

D.S. al Coda • Go back to the sign (𝄋), then play until the measure marked *"To Coda,"* then skip to the section labelled "**Coda.**"

D.C. al Fine • Go back to the beginning of the song and play until the measure marked *"Fine"* (end).

Rhy. Fig. • Label used to recall a recurring accompaniment pattern (usually chordal).

Riff • Label used to recall composed, melodic lines (usually single notes) which recur.

Fill • Label used to identify a brief melodic figure which is to be inserted into the arrangement.

Rhy. Fill • A chordal version of a Fill.

tacet • Instrument is silent (drops out).

• Repeat measures between signs.

• When a repeated section has different endings, play the first ending only the first time and the second ending only the second time.

NOTE: Tablature numbers in parentheses mean:
1. The note is being sustained over a system (note in standard notation is tied), or
2. The note is sustained, but a new articulation (such as a hammer-on, pull-off, slide or vibrato) begins, or
3. The note is a barely audible "ghost" note (note in standard notation is also in parentheses).

GUITAR RECORDED VERSIONS®

Guitar Recorded Versions® are note-for-note transcriptions of guitar music taken directly off recordings. This series, one of the most popular in print today, features some of the greatest guitar players and groups from blues and rock to country and jazz.

Guitar Recorded Versions are transcribed by the best transcribers in the business. Every book contains notes and tablature. Visit www.halleonard.com for our complete selection.

GUITAR *signature licks*

Signature Licks book/CD packs provide a step-by-step breakdown of "right from the record" riffs, licks, and solos so you can jam along with your favorite bands. They contain performance notes and an overview of each artist's or group's style, with note-for-note transcriptions in notes and tab. The CDs feature full-band demos at both normal and slow speeds.

ACOUSTIC CLASSICS
00695864 ....$19.95

AEROSMITH 1973-1979
00695106 ....$22.95

AEROSMITH 1979-1998
00695219 ....$22.95

BEST OF AGGRO-METAL
00695592 ....$19.95

DUANE ALLMAN
00696042 ....$22.99

BEST OF CHET ATKINS
00695752 ....$22.95

THE BEACH BOYS DEFINITIVE COLLECTION
00695683 ....$22.95

BEST OF THE BEATLES FOR ACOUSTIC GUITAR
00695453 ....$22.95

THE BEATLES BASS
00695283 ....$22.95

THE BEATLES FAVORITES
00695096 ....$24.95

THE BEATLES HITS
00695049 ....$24.95

BEST OF GEORGE BENSON
00695418 ....$22.95

BEST OF BLACK SABBATH
00695249 ....$22.95

BEST OF BLINK - 182
00695704 ....$22.95

BLUES BREAKERS WITH JOHN MAYALL & ERIC CLAPTON
00696374 ....$22.99

BEST OF BLUES GUITAR
00695846 ....$19.95

BLUES GUITAR CLASSICS
00695177 ....$19.95

BLUES/ROCK GUITAR HEROES
00696381 ....$19.99

BLUES/ROCK GUITAR MASTERS
00695348 ....$21.95

KENNY BURRELL
00695830 ....$22.99

BEST OF CHARLIE CHRISTIAN
00695584 ....$22.95

BEST OF ERIC CLAPTON
00695038 ....$24.95

ERIC CLAPTON – THE BLUESMAN
00695040 ....$22.95

ERIC CLAPTON – FROM THE ALBUM UNPLUGGED
00695250 ....$24.95

BEST OF CREAM
00695251 ....$22.95

CREEDANCE CLEARWATER REVIVAL
00695924 ....$22.95

DEEP PURPLE – GREATEST HITS
00695625 ....$22.95

THE BEST OF DEF LEPPARD
00696516 ....$22.95

THE DOORS
00695373 ....$22.95

TOMMY EMMANUEL
00696409 ....$22.99

ESSENTIAL JAZZ GUITAR
00695875 ....$19.99

FAMOUS ROCK GUITAR SOLOS
00695590 ....$19.95

ROBBEN FORD
00695903 ....$22.95

GREATEST GUITAR SOLOS OF ALL TIME
00695301 ....$19.95

BEST OF GRANT GREEN
00695747 ....$22.95

BEST OF GUNS N' ROSES
00695183 ....$24.95

THE BEST OF BUDDY GUY
00695186 ....$22.99

JIM HALL
00695848 ....$22.99

HARD ROCK SOLOS
00695591 ....$19.95

JIMI HENDRIX
00696560 ....$24.95

JIMI HENDRIX – VOLUME 2
00695835 ....$24.95

JOHN LEE HOOKER
00695894 ....$19.99

HOT COUNTRY GUITAR
00695580 ....$19.95

BEST OF JAZZ GUITAR
00695586 ....$24.95

ERIC JOHNSON
00699317 ....$24.95

ROBERT JOHNSON
00695264 ....$22.95

BARNEY KESSEL
00696009 ....$22.99

THE ESSENTIAL ALBERT KING
00695713 ....$22.95

B.B. KING – THE DEFINITIVE COLLECTION
00695635 ....$22.95

B.B. KING – MASTER BLUESMAN
00699923 ....$24.99

THE KINKS
00695553 ....$22.95

BEST OF KISS
00699413 ....$22.95

MARK KNOPFLER
00695178 ....$22.95

LYNYRD SKYNYRD
00695872 ....$24.95

BEST OF PAT MARTINO
00695632 ....$24.99

WES MONTGOMERY
00695387 ....$24.95

BEST OF NIRVANA
00695483 ....$24.95

THE OFFSPRING
00695852 ....$24.95

VERY BEST OF OZZY OSBOURNE
00695431 ....$22.95

BRAD PAISLEY
00696379 ....$22.99

BEST OF JOE PASS
00695730 ....$22.95

TOM PETTY
00696021 ....$22.99

PINK FLOYD – EARLY CLASSICS
00695566 ....$22.95

THE POLICE
00695724 ....$22.95

THE GUITARS OF ELVIS
00696507 ....$22.95

BEST OF QUEEN
00695097 ....$24.95

BEST OF RAGE AGAINST THE MACHINE
00695480 ....$24.95

RED HOT CHILI PEPPERS
00695173 ....$22.95

RED HOT CHILI PEPPERS – GREATEST HITS
00695828 ....$24.95

BEST OF DJANGO REINHARDT
00695660 ....$24.95

BEST OF ROCK
00695884 ....$19.95

ROCK BAND
00696063 ....$22.99

BEST OF ROCK 'N' ROLL GUITAR
00695559 ....$19.95

BEST OF ROCKABILLY GUITAR
00695785 ....$19.95

THE ROLLING STONES
00695079 ....$24.95

BEST OF DAVID LEE ROTH
00695843 ....$24.95

BEST OF JOE SATRIANI
00695216 ....$22.95

BEST OF SILVERCHAIR
00695488 ....$22.95

THE BEST OF SOUL GUITAR
00695703 ....$19.95

BEST OF SOUTHERN ROCK
00695560 ....$19.95

STEELY DAN
00696015 ....$22.99

MIKE STERN
00695800 ....$24.99

BEST OF SURF GUITAR
00695822 ....$19.95

BEST OF SYSTEM OF A DOWN
00695788 ....$22.95

ROBIN TROWER
00695950 ....$22.95

STEVE VAI
00673247 ....$22.95

STEVE VAI – ALIEN LOVE SECRETS: THE NAKED VAMPS
00695223 ....$22.95

STEVE VAI – FIRE GARDEN: THE NAKED VAMPS
00695166 ....$22.95

STEVE VAI – THE ULTRA ZONE: NAKED VAMPS
00695684 ....$22.95

STEVIE RAY VAUGHAN – 2ND ED.
00699316 ....$24.95

THE GUITAR STYLE OF STEVIE RAY VAUGHAN
00695155 ....$24.95

BEST OF THE VENTURES
00695772 ....$19.95

THE WHO – 2ND ED.
00695561 ....$22.95

JOHNNY WINTER
00695951 ....$22.99

BEST OF ZZ TOP
00695738 ....$24.95

HAL•LEONARD® CORPORATION
7777 W. BLUEMOUND RD. P.O. BOX 13819
MILWAUKEE, WISCONSIN 53213

www.halleonard.com

COMPLETE DESCRIPTIONS AND SONGLISTS ONLINE!
Prices, contents and availability subject to change without notice.

0811